A 21-DAY POETIC DEVOTIONAL
of God's Love & Grace

Respiration

THROUGH THE SEASONS OF LIFE

I0458373

STEPHANIE SALINAS ROMAN

Copyright© 2024 by Stephanie Salinas Roman
Cover design by Jennifer Gunn, Graphic Artist

Scripture quotations are taken from the Holy Bible, New Living Translation, (NLT) Copyright© 1996, 2004, 2007, 2013, 2015 by Tyndale House Foundation. Used by permission of Tyndale House Publishers, Inc., Carol Stream, Illinois 60188. All rights reserved.

Scripture quotations marked (NIV) are taken from the Holy Bible, New International Version®, NIV®. Copyright© 1973, 1978, 1984, 2011 by Biblica, Inc.™ Used by permission of Zondervan. All rights reserved worldwide. www. zondervan.com.
The "NIV" and "New International Version" are trademarks registered in the United States Patent and Trademark Office by Biblica, Inc.™

Scripture quotations are from Revised Standard Version (RSV) of the Bible, Copyright© 1946, 1952, and 1971 National Council of the Churches of Christ in the United States of America. Used by permission. All rights reserved worldwide.

Scripture quotations are from the ESV® Bible (The Holy Bible, English Standard Version®), copyright© 2001 by Crossway, a publishing ministry of Good News Publishers. Used by permission. All rights reserved."

Scripture quotations are taken from the New King James Version®.
Copyright© 1982 by Thomas Nelson. Used by permission. All rights reserved.

Scripture quotations marked "KJV" are taken from the Holy Bible, King James Version (Public Domain).

Scripture quotations marked NIRV® are taken from the Holy Bible, NEW INTERNATIONAL READER'S VERSION®. Copyright© 1996, 1998 Biblica. All rights reserved throughout the world. Used by permission of Biblica.

No part of this book may be reproduced or transmitted in any form or by any electronic or mechanical means, including photocopying, recording, or by any information storage and retrieval system, without the written permission of the publisher, except where permitted by law.

ISBN: 9781958032213

A product of the United States of America. This book is a work of non-fiction.

HERE I AM
PUBLISHING, LLC

Sandra Huddleston-Edwards, Publisher
780 Monterrosa Drive
Myrtle Beach, SC 29572
704 604 7265

DEDICATION

To my nieces and nephews,
I love you all so much!

Believe and trust God in all that you do!

Love, Tia Funny

ACKNOWLEDGEMENTS

I want to begin by expressing my deepest gratitude to God for guiding me through His perfect will all these years. Thank you, Jesus, and the Holy Spirit for inspiring my words.

To my siblings—Angel, Yesenia, Vida, Jennifer, Jessica, Crystal, and Jesse—your unwavering belief and support of my writing journey means the world to me.

To my mom, Maria, your love and courage during your darkest times inspired me to never give up on my dreams. Thank you for introducing me to faith as a young child and keeping our family close to God.

With a full heart, I acknowledge my husband, Sean; my children; and my family. You all have been an invaluable source of encouragement as I completed this divine assignment.

To my life coach, Myla, your mentorship, prayers, and support have been instrumental in my journey to healing through my relationship with God.

To all my mentors, friends, and sisters in Christ, thank you for your continuous support and prayers.

Finally, a heartfelt thank you to Sandi Huddleston-Edwards of Here I Am Publishing for offering a platform for Christian writers like myself to share God's love with the world.

CONTENTS

FORWARD

As founder of Forgiven Ministry, I have the privilege to speak in many places that want to learn about prison ministry. I was speaking to an NC law firm, which had filled the conference room with employees. I noticed a young lady who seemed to understand every word with such an interest in every word I spoke. After speaking, I gathered my things to leave the meeting, and the young lady followed me to my car. She could only get out, "I want to help you in prison ministry." I knew with her response she had experienced some form of incarceration in her life. I later learned that her stepfather had been incarcerated, which enabled her to understand the mission of Forgiven Ministry.

It was not long until Stephanie volunteered at a Georgia One Day with God Camp. I watched Stephanie all day, and it was evident she was filled with compassion and love to share with others. At the NC Nash Correctional One Day with God Camp, I made a point to spend some time with her, and she shared that she loved to write poetry. I asked to read one of her poems, which was about her mother, entitled "Her Hands Hold Much." I read it repeatedly, and my heart was so touched. The tears would not quit coming for it was as if she was writing about my grandmother.

Stephanie writes from her heart and experiences in life. As you read *Respiration*, you, too, will find poems that bring back memories of your life. Stephanie's poetry is guided by her Savior and her love to relate to others. I am so proud to tell you that Stephanie Roman serves on the Forgiven Ministry Board and attends each event she can. She has a gift of listening to God and letting Him guide her in His time and His will. As you read each selection, ask the Lord to speak to your heart just as He spoke to Stephanie's heart as she wrote *Respiration*.

Scottie Barnes, Founder

Forgiven Ministry, Inc.

INTRODUCTION

Welcome to *Respiration*, a 21-day poetic devotional and prayer journey where I invite you, friend, to embrace poetry and prayer as a form of worship and praise unto the Lord. The title *Respiration* was laid on my heart in 2019, when I was going through a difficult season, and through prayers and a personal relationship with God, I was finally able to breathe once I surrendered my life to my Abba Father.

This collection of poems was birthed from painful failed relationships, family memories, my relationship with God, inner healing, finding my identity in Christ Jesus, and lots of crying and praying for loved ones, friends, and myself. It was a long journey of stillness, singleness, and surrendering it all to God.

According to *Merriam-Webster Dictionary*, the definition of "respiration" is "a single complete act of breathing." It was the breath of God in me that gave me life and kept me alive all these years for such a time as this. In allowing God to lead me and guide my steps, *Respiration* became my first poetry book project with Him.

I prayed and prayed for

- the words to write,
- Him to send the right publisher for me,
- those who would read this book, and
- my work to bring Him glory.

My hope is that your prayer life will be strengthened through this 21-day poetic devotional and prayer journey.

TOPICS

As you start reading *Respiration*, I pray and hope that you will be immersed in a journey and prayer life where God will open your heart to experience the world around you in a different way. The poems' topics include God's love and grace, grief, mother's love, womanhood, freedom from addictions, friendships, strength, courage, healing, and hope. May your life be transformed through His grace and love toward you.

VERSES AND PRAYERS

Each poem has a corresponding prayer and Bible verse. Take a few minutes after reading the poem to pray and meditate on the scripture, opening your heart to let the Lord bring you what you may need that day. God loves to surprise us!

REFLECTION

I invite you to start journaling your 21-day poetic devotional and prayer journey. It may not seem like many words are written out at the beginning or maybe the floodgates will open as soon as you start Day 1. However your journey starts, don't stop writing it out. Let the Holy Spirit guide you day by day. You will be amazed by the end of the 21-day journey, and you may even find that you, yourself, are a poet too. God gives us all gifts and talents. Sometimes, they are just hidden under layers of pain. Only until we walk alongside God with a surrendered spirit can He do in us to whom He called us to be.

I am thankful for your support, and I pray that God continues to build you up as you grow in your relationship with Him. Keep praying, Prayer Warrior!

All for God's glory, I am

Stephanie

DAY I:

RESPIRATION

DAY 1:

RESPIRATION

Renew our mind, oh God.

Like a flowing stream of water
Let your Holy Spirit bring forth
Fresh understanding of your Word.

God transform our lives
Like that of a tree through seasons
Peeling away the old
To bring forth a new creation.

Though the winds of life
May blow through our bodies
The breath of God keeps us
Grounded in His presence.

Blood vessels like roots
Buried deep into our bodies
Holy Spirit guard our souls.

Like branches on a tree
We are connected to God
Through His Son,
Jesus Christ, our Savior.
Breathe into us Your gift of life
So that we may live
In your peace and love daily.

The title poem, "Respiration," was written during the Covid-19 pandemic and during one of the hardest seasons of my life, where I found myself drawing closer to the Lord through prayer and solitude. It was a season of surrendering all to Him and learning to just breathe in His gift of life. It was a nine-month process of prayer and asking the Holy Spirit to guide me in writing this poem that connected my life to that of nature. My love for nature will always be reflected in my poetry. It's God's most beautiful creation.

Bible Verse:

"Do not be conformed to this world, but be transformed by the renewal of your mind, that by testing you may discern what is the will of God, what is good and acceptable and perfect"
(Romans 12:2, ESV).

This bible verse reflects the poem, "Respiration's" theme of renewing our body and mind so that we may grow through each season of our lives. It's a reminder to never stay stagnant in one's own thoughts, but to align them with the Word of God.

Prayer:

Dear Abba Father,

Thank You for leading me closer to You. Help me to be patient in the process and to stop and pray about everything in my life that is going on around me. I am a vessel for Your Kingdom--I surrender to Your will. Move me. Prepare me for Your works. Renew my body, mind, and soul so that I am stronger each day to walk in Your peace and favor. Pull out the weeds from my life that give no good fruit, and pour into my heart that which is good and from You.

In Jesus name, I pray. Amen.

Reflection

DAY 1:

_____

_____

_____

_____

_____

_____

_____

_____

_____

_____

_____

_____

_____

_____

_____

_____

_____

_____

DAY 2:

A LETTER TO
MY CREATOR

DAY 2:

A LETTER TO MY CREATOR

Dear God,

Thank You for creating me
The almighty Creator of all.
You had a purpose for me.

You knew me before I came to be.
I was destined to be here.
You had Your hands protecting me.

Before birth and after
Your love covers me.
The greatest love of all.

My God, my first love,
My Creator,

I'm forever grateful
To be a life that matters to You.

Love Always,

Your child

Through my healing journey, I learned that I was loved by my heavenly Father and that as a Child of God, I mattered to Him. In writing the poem, "A Letter to My Creator," I am expressing my gratitude for being alive here on Earth for a purpose. It's a love letter from a child to her Father. We all have a Father who loves us so much.

Bible Verse:

"Before I formed you in the womb, I knew you, before you were born I set you apart; I appointed you as a prophet to the nations"
(Jeremiah 1:5, NIV).

This Bible verse is powerful in that it shows us how much God intended for us to be born for a purpose. No matter if you were rejected or unwanted before or after birth, God already knew you and formed you. He formed you for His purpose, and when we know our identity in Christ Jesus, nothing can steal our God-given purpose.

Prayer:

Dear Abba Father,

Thank You for this beautiful day ahead of me, the day You created for me to experience Your goodness and favor. Thank You for creating me for such a time as this. You knew me before I was born; You knew my name, my personality, my skills, and my talents. All of that You knew because You created me for a special purpose here on Earth. Lead me on the right path that You have for me. Thank You for loving me yesterday, today, and always. Draw me closer to You each and every day of my life.

In Jesus name, I pray. Amen.

Reflection

DAY 2:

_____

_____

_____

_____

_____

_____

_____

_____

_____

_____

_____

_____

_____

_____

_____

_____

_____

_____

DAY 3:

CARELESS

DAY 3:

CARELESS

You give and take away.
To your knees you pray.

Help me, God!
Get me through this day.

Shadows linger through the dark.
A careless whisper tears your heart.

Give me strength my Lord.
Hold me through this door.

Wake my soul.

During a stressful day at work and the pressure of
personal challenges, I wrote the poem "Careless," as a
way to release my pain and emotions in that moment
where I felt helpless and defeated by life. I needed
help, like so many of us do in times of hardships
and unplanned delays. Only God can help us in our
deepest moments of despair.

Bible Verse:

"Have I not commanded you? Be strong and of good courage; do not be afraid, nor be dismayed, for the Lord your God is with you wherever you go"
(Joshua 1:9, NKJV).

This is one of the Bible verses I pray when I feel overwhelmed by the challenges of life. It is one that gives me strength to keep going, not letting fear or discouragement get me off track.

Prayer:

Dear Abba Father,

Forgive me for my sins. Thank You for another new day. Help me get through this day. Help me not to feel overwhelmed. Your will be done. Help me to let go and trust Your plan for my life. Help me to not be afraid to move forward with my life. Hold me in Your perfect love through this journey of life.

In Jesus name, I pray. Amen.

Reflection

DAY 3:

_____

_____

_____

_____

_____

_____

_____

_____

_____

_____

_____

_____

_____

_____

_____

_____

_____

_____

DAY 4:

THE PATH

DAY 4:

THE PATH

The breeze hits your face; you're alive,
Walking down a path that you'll survive.

Trees blooming; it's a sign, a new season.
Breathe in and love this path with reason.

Fresh water flowing through the stream.
Renew yourself; let your soul beam.

The path of life ever-winding but beautiful.
Take a leap of faith and be purposeful.

During a season after a broken relationship and
learning to navigate life as a single woman, the poem,
"The Path," was inspired after a sunny spring day
walk in the park to help me release my emotions and
tears. By taking long walks in nature or sitting by
the pond in silence, I slowly began to feel peace and
God's love all around me. It was a reminder that it was
going to be okay. This new journey I was on was for a
purpose, and I would survive. I did.

Bible Verse:

"Your Word is a Lamp to my feet and a light to my path"
(Psalm 119:105, NKJV).

I love that God's Word guides our every step. Even if we get off track, He still lights the path for us to walk in His will. We are never too far from His grace and mercy. This Bible verse helped me when I felt alone and didn't know which way to go or if I was going down the right path. Through prayer, God kept His light shining over my life.

Prayer:

Dear Abba Father,

Thank You for this new day and season of my life. Thank You for healing my body, mind, and soul. Thank You for my family and friends. Thank You for providing all my needs during this journey. Lead me, Lord, through this path of a new season of my life. Give me peace and strength as I take the leap of faith and continue following Your will for my life. My hope is in You Lord each and every day. I love You.

In Jesus name, I pray. Amen.

Reflection

DAY 4:

DAY 5:

FAMILIAR PLACES, OLD FACES

FAMILIAR PLACES, OLD FACES

Riding down memory lane with a friend,
It was familiar places and old faces.

The empty seats are filled up streets,
Bittersweet memories filled with beats.

Conversations with a familiar face,
Listening to music to set the pace.

Change can be good for you,
But is it good for them or for who?

Broken relationships with tainted hearts,
An open dialogue about faded starts.

Finding peace in empty spaces,
When it's over with familiar places.

It was understanding and patience,
That not everything would be gracious.

Finding God, and like the lyric stated,
To press forward in life, don't give up.

It was music and time to ease the mind.
Familiar places, old faces.

On a Sunday afternoon after a meaningful visit from a childhood friend, the poem, "Familiar Places, Old Faces," was inspired. I was encouraged that I wasn't alone in my experiences of a broken relationship or heartache and that there was hope at the end of all the broken pieces. I wasn't ashamed of the failed relationship anymore and that I could be the woman God created me to be, to share my testimony of hope and love with others.

Bible Verse:

"There is no greater love than to lay down one's life for one's friends"
(John 15:13, NLT).

This Bible verse reminds me of the importance of being a friend to all--to encourage and serve those in need, and to put other's needs before myself in order to glorify God. I am grateful for those I can call friends.

Prayer:

Dear Abba Father,

Thank You for another glorious day in Your presence. Thank You for the friendships in my life, the ones You have sustained and protected for years. Help me to be more kind and loving to serve those around me with a grateful heart. Help me to know the good friends that surround me and to discern those who may not be a friend to pray for them and protect myself, as well. Thank You, Jesus Christ, for being my best friend. Thank You for Your love and the life You gave for all of us. Thank you, God, for sending Your only Son to die for me, for calling me a friend. I am thankful today for knowing that You are my friend.

In Jesus name, I pray. Amen.

Reflection

DAY 5:

_____

_____

_____

_____

_____

_____

_____

_____

_____

_____

_____

_____

_____

_____

_____

_____

_____

_____

DAY 6:

BABY SOUL

DAY 6:

BABY SOUL

(For my loving sister Crystal, forever inspired by your courage)

My fist hit the
Jagged porch railing.
To my knees I fell.
Why God?

Crying out to my God,
Letting it out, finally,
From days of disbelief.
It all happened so fast.

A tragic accident
Left our close-knit
Family devastated
With broken hearts.

My little sister's first born
Baby, a sweet loving boy
Christian, forever
We love you.

It was the joy of planning
A baby shower to
Heartbreaking conversations
Of picking songs
For a memorial service.
Staying strong for my

Little sister.
Holding back my tears.
Sitting on her living room floor
As if it were just another
Family gathering.

My little sister,
Said goodbye forever
With courage so
Unbelievable
To her sweet baby boy.

My mother, oh if
I could take her pain
Away.
Her grandbaby's
Little feet no longer
In her garden.

A baby soul taken too soon.
Fly high our angel baby boy.

The first death in my immediate family was my
little sister's first child, Christian Ivan. Watching
everyone process his death was painful after leaving
the hospital. I didn't cry at the hospital because I had
to stay strong for everyone else. My sister, a miracle
baby herself, gracefully grieved his death. I admire her
strength as a mother. I wrote "Baby Soul," in loving
memory of my baby nephew whom we all love so
much and miss every day.

Bible Verse:

*"'The Lord is my portion,' says my soul, 'Therefore
I hope in Him'"
(Lamentations 3:24, NKJV)!*

In the uncertainty of life events through death and
heartaches, this Bible verse reminds me to place my
hope in the Lord. The most certain things we have are
God's love and peace.

Prayer:

Dear Abba Father,

Thank You for Your peace in times of pain and
heartache. In seasons of grief and tears, Lord we know
that our HOPE is in You. We can come to You and
find rest during a time of stillness in our life where
words cannot mend a broken heart. Only Your love
can wrap us up in Your arms and carry us through the
days of sorrow. Thank You for giving us families and
friends to share our heartaches with and to cry and
pray together. Thank You for mothers. Thank You for
my sister, a miracle baby, a walking testimony of Your
unfailing love and favor.

In Jesus name, I pray. Amen.

Reflection

DAY 6:

_____

_____

_____

_____

_____

_____

_____

_____

_____

_____

_____

_____

_____

_____

_____

_____

_____

RESTORATION

DAY 7:

RESTORATION

Unchained
and
unclaimed by
drugs.

No one
knows their
story.

The cyclones
in their mind.

Shadows linger
injecting
fear in them.

A soul free from
the streets,
a life of
defeats.

A fighter you survived
redeeming your life,
no longer deprived.

It's a
lifetime gained,
a soul
no longer
chained.

No, it's just
NOT
years.

Its generational
restoration.

Only God can
restore the broken.

Watching loved ones and friends go through the
cycle of drug addiction is devastating, with feelings of
helplessness and worry for their lives daily. However,
there is hope in recovery and restoring one's life
from addiction, and it's a beautiful transformation to
be a part of seeing how God can change a person's
life for His glory. There are powerful testimonies in
the stories of those who have overcome addiction,
and it's important to share them to help others find
freedom, too. You can make a difference. The poem,
"Restoration," is a dedication to those who have
overcome addictions. May you know you are not
alone, and God is our healer.

Bible Verse:

Therefore, if anyone is in Christ, the new creation has come:
The old has gone, the new is here"
(2 Corinthians 5:17, NIV)!

Becoming who God created us to be is a transformation and growth process. However, there is joy in knowing that once we are saved, the person we used to be is no longer who we are. Our identity is now in Christ Jesus; we are a new person, restored and healed for His glory. This Bible verse encourages us to know who we are in Christ all the days of our life.

Prayer:

Dear Abba Father,

I come to You, Father, adopted into Your royal family and no longer chained to my past or addictions that go against Your Holy Word. Forgive me for my sins of self-harm to my body and of thoughts that are not of You. Help me, Holy Spirit, to honor my body in a way that brings glory to God, my heavenly Father. Help me to be mindful of my thoughts and actions. Help me to pray in the moments of despair. Help me to grow in the fruits of the Spirit. Help me to love myself as You love me, Jesus. Restore my life, lead me, and build me up for Your kingdom's works.

In Jesus name, I pray. Amen.

Reflection

DAY 7:

_____

_____

_____

_____

_____

_____

_____

_____

_____

_____

_____

_____

_____

_____

_____

_____

_____

_____

DAY 8:

HER HANDS
HOLD MUCH

DAY 8:

HER HANDS HOLD MUCH

I see my mother's hands,
Fragile yet strong,
Holding generations of wisdom
And love.

Holding her Bible, she prays.
Holding her needle, she sews.
Holding her seeds, she plants.

I see my mother's hands.
Wrinkles from years of labor
Holding the tears of her
Children.

Holding her apron, she cooks.
Holding her broom, she cleans.
Holding her pen, she writes.

I see my mother's hands
Holding so much, passing
Her years of wisdom to
Her daughters.

For we are our mothers'
Seeds, women whose
Hands hold much.

This poem is dedicated to my mother, Maria Del Rosario, in gratitude for all that she has done for us while we were growing up. This is an expression of love to show that I've seen her sacrifices for our family, and I'm thankful for her heart to serve those around her. I love you, Ma.

Bible Verse:

"She is clothed with strength and dignity; she can laugh at the days to come"
(Proverbs 31:25, NIV).

This Bible verse is a favorite of mine to remind me of who I am as a woman of God. I think of my mom when I read this verse, and when I need inspiration as a wife and mother, I read Proverbs 31 to be encouraged and to also encourage other women. We are all sisters in Christ, and supporting each other is important.

Prayer:

Dear Abba Father,

Thank You for creating my mother and her mother and her mother and her mother—we are all connected to Jesus' mother—Mary. Thank You for a mother's love that You created us all to experience through her labor pains. Thank You for the women who are our spiritual mothers—mothers to many near and far who give without asking and love without barriers. I pray for all our mothers; may you give them the strength and courage to continue to raise children who fear You and worship and seek Your face all the days of their lives.

In Jesus name, I pray. Amen.

Reflection

DAY 8:

_____

_____

_____

_____

_____

_____

_____

_____

_____

_____

_____

_____

_____

_____

_____

_____

_____

DAY 9:

PHASES

DAY 9:

PHASES

If you love God's creation at its simplest form through
All its phases
You learn something from each phase.

Such are plants, simply and uniquely created
Each to a leaf so different
Yet so beautiful as simple as it may look.

From the seeds to repotting them
For space to grow bigger
Plants embrace change.

To love a plant is to love the flower
Before the flower was yet to be.

Many want a flower but only while
It stays alive and pretty,
Yet don't know how to
Take care of a simple plant.

Plants embrace patience and brokenness
For if a stem breaks,
The plant will re-grow a new one.

We must be patient through the valley,
For when we are broken
We too will grow stronger each time.

As a plant lover, I enjoy watching the process of life and phases through them. This poem was written as a reminder to embrace each phase of our lives as we grow and break through the seasons of life. It's a beautiful process to grow and learn from each phase of life. God created us to grow, too.

Bible Verse:

"So neither the one who plants nor the one who waters is anything, but only God, who makes things grow"
(1 Corinthians 3:7, NIV).

This Bible verse encourages me to stay humble in that only through God can we grow through our seasons of life.

Prayer:

Dear Abba Father,

You are the Creator of all the plants and flowers in the universe. Thank You for allowing me to embrace the beauty of life through plants and to embrace change and growth. Thank You for being patient and loving toward me as I grow closer to You like a plant. I, too, need Your living water to give me life. Help me to embrace all the phases of my life and enjoy the moments through the journey You have already set before me.

In Jesus name, I pray. Amen.

Reflection

DAY 9:

_____

_____

_____

_____

_____

_____

_____

_____

_____

_____

_____

_____

_____

_____

_____

_____

_____

_____

DAY 10:
A POET'S MOTTO

A POET'S MOTTO

Poetry--
Inked emotions
Calming the soul
Words deeply paint art
--Passion.

As a poet, expressing my feelings through words comes naturally. I am so grateful to God for the gift of writing and being able to encourage others through my writing. This poem is a dedication to all the poets: May you continue to paint the world with your words.

Bible Verse:

"Then the Lord replied: 'Write down the revelation and make it plain on tablets so that a herald may run with it'" *(Habakkuk 2:2, NIV).*

When I read this Bible verse, it was evident that God wants us to use our gifts as writers to keep a journal and write our vision, goals, prayers, poems, letters, stories, etc. Writing is a love language, and when you are a writer, it's important to share your story with others through the words given to you by the Holy Spirit.

Prayer:

Dear Abba Father,

Thank You for this beautiful day that You created. Thank You for allowing me to witness to others through the words on these pages. I pray that they bring healing and encouragement to every person who reads through this devotional. I pray that those seeking to know their purpose and passion will seek it through You and that You will give them clarity and a vision of Your will for their life as you have helped me in finding my purpose through poetry.

In Jesus name, I pray. Amen

Reflection

DAY 10:

_____

_____

_____

_____

_____

_____

_____

_____

_____

_____

_____

_____

_____

_____

_____

_____

_____

_____

DAY II:

SPEAK LIFE

DAY II:

SPEAK LIFE

Silence of the
Morning dew,
Life is among you.

Lightness through the
Horizon on a foggy crispy
Winter's day.

Flowing through your body
A cellular connection
To the universe.

God's miraculous
Beauty in everything.
Speak Life!

As a teenager, I understood the power of life and death
through our words when thoughts of not wanting to
be alive entered my mind one night. The next day on
the way to school, our bus was involved in an accident
with an 18-wheeler. As I was praying on the bus, as
I always did, I felt the impact and heard the glass
shatter. However, God's Hand protected me in that
moment, and I was not harmed. I never spoke of death
over my life again. The life we are given is a gift from

God, and we should honor His love for us each day we are breathing here on Earth. The poem, "Speak Life," was written to encourage those who may be having suicidal thoughts to know that there is hope and to speak life, to live, to feel the connection around you and to embrace God's gift of life.

Bible Verse:

"Death and life are in the power of the tongue, and they who indulge in it shall eat the fruit of it [for death or life]" (Proverbs 18:21, AMPC).

As we grow in Christ, we begin to understand the power behind our thoughts and words. It's important that we renew our mind through the Word of God in order that we may start speaking life into every aspect of our lives. Speak encouraging words, words that build up and bring about hope and love. This Bible verse holds much truth about how to be mindful of our words.

Prayer:

Dear Abba Father,

Thank You for Your breath of life. I pray for those who are experiencing a dry season in their lives and who may feel down or depressed. I speak life over those reading this poem. I lift them up in prayer. Please break every chain that keeps them in darkness and bondage from enjoying life. Free them now. They will live and not die. I declare life over them from the top of their heads to the bottom of their feet. Revive them and breathe life into them again. Thank You because their lives matter to You.

In Jesus name, I pray. Amen

Reflection

DAY II:

_____

_____

_____

_____

_____

_____

_____

_____

_____

_____

_____

_____

_____

_____

_____

_____

_____

DAY 12:

WALK IN IT

DAY 12:

WALK IN IT

In the fire of pain
Burning through fears
Shadows of black ashes
Lost in smoke--

Walk In It.

In the death of the past
Buried through tears
Survivor of hurts
Love in brokenness--

Walk In It.

In the Breath of Life
Born through His Love
Saved by His Grace
Light in darkness--

Walk In It.

For the Holy Spirit is with you.

In 2021, during the Covid 19 pandemic, I was faced with a season of being unemployed, and I prayed for God's guidance in an unfamiliar territory of being single and unemployed for the first time as an adult. I sought the Lord, I drew closer to Him, and I walked in faith. I began to find peace and healing in my daily prayer and worship time, where many of my prayers and poems were birthed from a time of many tears and doubting myself, but I knew God's Word was true, and I believed He would see me through that season as He always has. And He did. The poem, "Walk In It," was my 2021 anthem poem. I walked into a new season that year for God's glory.

Bible Verse:

"…but those who hope in the Lord will renew their strength. They will soar on wings like eagles; they will run and not grow weary, they will walk and not be faint"
Isaiah 40:31 (NIV).

As we walk in faith, we will get weary, but this Bible verse promises that God will renew our strength when we place our hope in Him and not the world or the situation. It's a constant reminder to focus on our Lord daily and not let our hardships bring us down.

Prayer:

Dear Abba Father,

Thank You for this new day full of Your love, peace, and joy. You are working on my behalf. I walk in Your authority, knowing that You go before me. Your favor and grace cover me in each season of my life. I trust You with each step I take into my divine purpose that only You created me to fulfill for such a time as this. I praise You and give You glory for Your timing. I am never alone,; for that I am forever grateful.

In Jesus name, I pray. Amen

Reflection

DAY 12:

_____

_____

_____

_____

_____

_____

_____

_____

_____

_____

_____

_____

_____

_____

_____

_____

_____

_____

_____

_____

_____

DAY 13:

REFLECTIONS OF YOU

DAY 13:

REFLECTIONS OF YOU

Hold your head up high, my sister.
You are Peace, Love, and Strength.

Hold your head up high, my sister.
Peace and love are within you.
Be the light; be the love.

Hold your head up high, my sister.
Faith over fear, feel it, speak it.
Be bold, be fearless.

Hold your head up high, my sister.
Calm and relaxed, live it, breathe it.
Be in the moment, alive.

Hold your head up high, my sister.
You are Beauty, Wisdom, and Life.

Be the reflection that
God CREATED
You to be.

After a women's retreat and hearing the many stories of being set free from strongholds and healing from an abusive past as women, I wrote the poem, "Reflection of You," as a reminder to all women that we are created by a loving God and to walk in the authority as Women of God. There is a powerful and beautiful presence of the Lord when women come together in prayer and fellowship; never forget to be a sister in Christ to those around you, and remind each other to hold their heads up high as daughters of the Most High.

Bible Verse:

"Create in me a pure heart, O God, and renew a steadfast spirit within me"
(Psalm 51:10, NIV).

When God begins to transform our lives, He softens our heart and changes us from whom we used to be for His glory. It is through the Word of God that we can have a firm foundation of who we are in Christ and walk in that with confidence. This Bible verse helps us know we can come to God and ask for His help as we grow in our faith.

Prayer:

Dear Abba Father,

Today I come as a daughter to Your throne, giving You praise and worship for creating me anew through my salvation. Change in me, Lord, what is not pleasing to You. Create in me a new heart, a heart that reflects Your love, peace, and strength. Keep me in Your abundant love in this moment of my life. No matter the situation I may face, I know that I can be still in Your love and peace. I am becoming the woman You have anointed to share Your goodness with those around me. Prepare me for Your great works in my life. Thank you, Lord.

In Jesus name, I pray. Amen

Reflection

DAY 13:

DAY 14:

HOLD MY HANDS, NOT YOUR THOUGHTS

DAY 14:

HOLD MY HAND, NOT YOUR THOUGHTS

My dearest friend, words will never be enough to free you from the pain, to free you from your thoughts that spin out of control at times. I see myself in you, the fragile soul we all become in a life of misfortunes. You are not alone in this battle. I will fight with you. Through tears and prayers, I'll be there for you. Through laughs and smiles, I'll shine the light on you. Through days and nights, I'll be thinking about you.

I'll hold your hand,
To remind you that with a small act of kindness, you are not alone.

I'll hold your hand,
To remind you that your heart still beats to the rhythm of life's precious moments.

I'll hold your hand,
To remind you that the stars and the moon are like your sweet touch.

I'll hold your hand,
To remind you that the space between two souls is always small compared to the universe.

I'll hold your hand,
To remind you that you are special and your
fingerprints can't be replaced.

I'll hold your hand,
To remind you that you were created by a loving God
who holds you close to Him.

I'll hold your hand,
To remind you that you may hold much inside, but I'm
here to carry it with you.

I'll hold your hand,
To remind you to hold my hand when your thoughts
become too much.

Hold my hand, not your thoughts, my friend.

Having a friend that comes alongside you as you deal
with mental struggles is a blessing. The poem, "Hold
My Hand, Not Your Thoughts" was inspired after
being that kind of friend to someone who needed to
hear encouraging words as he/she overcame mental
battles. It's a reminder to all of us to be the friend we
would want to have in times of difficulty. Never pass
up the opportunity to sit with friends facing hardships.
They need it even if they don't know how to verbalize
gratitude for your presence. Remember, they are
battling a lot in their minds.

Bible Verse:

"Therefore encourage one another and build one another up, just as you are doing".
1 Thessalonians 5:11(ESV)

The Bible is full of verses on how to treat each other. This Bible verse is my favorite regarding friendships and being the kind of friend that Jesus was. When we align our thoughts and actions according to the Word of God, it becomes easier to show compassion and love to others.

Prayer:

Dear Abba Father,

I thank You for Your Son Jesus Christ, showing us how to be a friend to those around us: to lend a helping hand, a shoulder to lean on, a hand to hold during life's most difficult moments. We all grow through pain and suffering. Lord, help me to be a friend like Jesus: to pray for the stranger under the bridge, to leave a sweet note for the waitress, to encourage the becoming artist. Remind me in my mundane life to pause and look around for the hurting and be a friend. I thank You for sending those same God-sent friends into my life when I needed a friend. I thank You for loving me and blessing me with divine appointments.

In Jesus name, I pray. Amen

PRAYER JOURNAL

Reflection

DAY 14:

DAY 15:

WE ARE HIS WORKMANSHIP

DAY 15:

WE ARE HIS WORKMANSHIP

To go where God says
To serve with purpose.

To do what God says
To obey with confidence.

To be silent as God says
To pray with boldness.

To show love as God says
To give with a generous heart.

To forgive as God says
To help your neighbor instead.

To spread the Word as God says
To win souls for the kingdom of God.

To set the captive free as God says
To lead the lost to Christ.

When I studied the meaning of Workmanship in
Ephesians 2:10, I found that in Greek it means *Poiema*

and is the origin of the English word *poem*, which means "that which is made" according to an online dictionary: *https://www.billmounce.com/greek-dictionary/poiema*. We were created by God for a divine purpose. This poem was inspired by the Bible verse, Ephesians 2:10.

Bible Verse:

"For we are God's handiwork, created in Christ Jesus to do good works, which God prepared in advance for us to do" (Ephesians 2:10, NIV).

As a poet, I love to read the Bible as it is filled with so much poetic language. This Bible verse is special as it speaks to my heart as a poet. I know that my calling is from my heavenly Father and is for good works here on Earth.

Prayer:

Dear Abba Father,

Thank You, heavenly Father, for Your unfailing love. Thank You for creating me, for knowing I would have a purpose in this life. Thank you so much for the gifts and talents You have given me to share with the world for Your glory. Guide me in the way that You have set forth before me. Help me to see You in all that is around me. Thank You for filling me with Your love and confidence to do great things that may be pleasing to You, oh Lord. Here I am. Use me for Your Kingdom.

In Jesus name, I pray. Amen.

Reflection

DAY 15:

_____

_____

_____

_____

_____

_____

_____

_____

_____

_____

_____

_____

_____

_____

_____

_____

_____

_____

DAY 16:

FREEDOM

DAY 16:

FREEDOM

Freedom from guilt and shame from the past,
No longer tied to strongholds.
Freedom in Christ is yours,
We have been justified by faith.
And so, He will also bring glory,
Through His sovereignty.
Holy Spirit empower us,
To walk in freedom every day.
Deliver us Lord,
Today and forever.

In March 2023, I woke up from a dream in which I heard the words "living waters ministry," and I had never heard those words before. I started to *Google* these words, and to my surprise, it was a healing retreat in North Carolina. I reached out to them to ask if someone needed prayer, not realizing that God was showing me the place He wanted me to go. Reading back through my prayer journal, my words for 2022 were *surrender* and *freedom*. God was already working in me and preparing me for what was to come.

And I prayed for months and also let fear keep me from going. However, in September 2023, I finally drove to this beautiful countryside retreat and experienced a weekend full of God's presence. I surrendered it all that weekend--the painful wounds of my past-- and I left full of joy and freedom. Driving back home I was full of the Holy Spirit, and laughter filled the air as I could not stop laughing from the joy in my heart. This poem, "Freedom," was inspired from that weekend. It's a reminder to follow the voice of God even if it doesn't make sense. Take that leap of faith; there is freedom on the other side of obedience.

Bible Verse:

"I will walk about in freedom, for I have sought out your precepts"
(Psalm 119:45, NIV).

This Bible verse is my constant reminder to not go back, to not return to the past where God has led me from to freedom. It reminds me to keep walking in His love and keeping the Word always in my heart and mind. It's a beautiful journey walking out our faith each day with our Lord and Savior.

Prayer:

Dear Abba Father,

Thank You for this new day to walk in Your peace and love. You alone are my Joy and Peace. I am loved and walk in freedom. Holy Spirit, teach me to be wise and discern the things of God when I read the Bible. Lord, I pray for this nation; protect our children. For our government, place in position those who uphold your truth in their hearts that we may all walk in freedom as a body of Christ.

In Jesus name, I pray. Amen.

Reflection

DAY 16: _____

_____

_____

_____

_____

_____

_____

_____

_____

_____

_____

_____

_____

_____

_____

_____

_____

_____

_____

DAY 17:

I SURRENDER

Forgiven

DAY 17:

I SURRENDER

Vanity

Like a thief to rob my joy,
that creeps up in mind.

Distrust

Like a thorn in my side,
bleeding out everywhere.

Rage

Like shattered glass,
jagged edges too sharp to touch.

In repentance, I kneel before You.
Forgive me, Lord.

On January 2, 2022, my first prayer journal entry was titled "My Life I Surrender to Your Will, Lord." Part of my prayer was "I surrender my life to You, all my wants, feelings, desires, I give it all to You. Just as other strong Christian women before have done and prayed, I too, want to live a life to bring You glory."

I then wrote the prayer written by Betty Scott Stam in *Betty Scott Stam, A Life of Surrender*:

"Lord, I give up my own plans and purposes, all my own desires, hopes and ambitions, and I accept Thy will for my life. I give up myself, my life, my all, utterly to Thee, to be Thine forever. I hand over to Thy keeping all of my friendships; all the people whom I love are to take second place in my heart. Fill me now and seal me with Thy Spirit. Work out Thy whole will in my life at any cost, for to me to live is Christ. Amen."

I was going through a season of my life when I knew God was dealing with my heart and drawing me closer to Him. It was a season of self-reflection as I spent time in prayer and worship, laying it all at the foot of the Cross and allowing God to heal me. And it was a season of experiencing losses for His purpose and plan. He had to strip me of everything to get me to a place where I would not be distracted by other voices.

Bible Verse:

"Do not be anxious about anything, but in every situation, by prayer and petition, with thanksgiving, present your requests to God. And the peace of God, which transcends all understanding, will guard your hearts and your minds in Christ Jesus"
(Philippians 4:67, NIV).

This Bible verse is a reminder that when we surrender to God's will, His peace will flow into our lives, and we can be reassured that we can come to Him in our hardest moments of life.

Prayer:

Dear Abba Father,

I thank You for allowing me to be aware of my feelings and attitudes so that I may reflect upon them and come to You for guidance. Holy Spirit, help me to be more like Jesus and less like my flesh. Help me to uproot these old thought patterns that do not define who I am as a new creation in Christ Jesus. Send mentors, praying partners, godly relationships so that I may grow closer to You through fellowship, prayer, and worship. Help me be still in prayer to listen to Your voice and to surrender all my flaws so that only You can do a new thing through me, surrendering it all to you. Give me a fresh anointing, fresh fire, and a hunger for Your Word to dwell inside of me all the days of my life.

In Jesus name, I pray. Amen.

Reflection

DAY 17:

_____

_____

_____

_____

_____

_____

_____

_____

_____

_____

_____

_____

_____

_____

_____

_____

_____

DAY 18:

GOD KEPT ME

DAY 18:

GOD KEPT ME

Alive
Before I was born
In childhood traumas
Arrows flying by my side.

God kept me

Alive
Before I spoke my first word
In unhealthy relationships,
Fear and shame by my side.

God kept me

Alive
Before I knew my identity in Christ
In declaring the Word of God
Angels by my side.

God Kept you, alive, my friend
For a divine purpose.

Inspired by Psalm 91, the poem "God Kept Me" is a testament to God's unfailing protection throughout my life. When we have a heart of gratitude for being alive, we can see God's hand in the smallest details of our lives. Being able to apply the Word of God to our lives is essential in growing closer to who we are as followers of Jesus Christ.

Bible Verse:

"A thousand may fall at your side, ten thousand at your right hand, but it will not come near you"
(Psalm 91:7, NIV).

As a teenager, I read Psalm 91 when I felt afraid. I always pray this verse over myself, my family, and my friends in times of severe storms, plagues, and other fear-ridden things of this world. Always remember that God's protection covers you.

Prayer:

Dear Abba Father,

Thank You, Father, for loving me. I want to express my gratitude for being Your child here on Earth. You have always kept me in every season of my life. Help me grow through this season. You alone know my destiny, and I leave my life in Your hands; I trust you, Lord. Thank You for sending people into my life throughout each season of my life to help me grow and learn. I am thankful for Your faithfulness. I praise You, Lord, even in this season of unknown, I know You won't leave me. I pray for those going through similar situations that they may find comfort in Your Word and know in their hearts that Your promises are forever. May You keep me still and pour Your love and peace over me right now. Holy Spirit, guide me and intercede on my behalf when words fail to come out of my mouth. I love you, Lord. Help me to walk in grace and love always.

In Jesus name, I pray. Amen.

Reflection

DAY 18:

_____

_____

_____

_____

_____

_____

_____

_____

_____

_____

_____

_____

_____

_____

_____

_____

_____

_____

_____

DAY 19:

WHO AM I

DAY 19:

WHO AM I?

Who am I? The voices creep in and out of my mind.

Doubt, fear, and oppression bind me in place.

My body paralyzed in time, but my mind escapes this world.

Thoughts enter without notice.

Who am I? I ask myself again, in my mind.
I am a child of God.
I am a loving and caring daughter, sister, wife, and mother.
I am a friend to many.
I am a caretaker.
I am an intelligent human being.
I am sensitive to other's needs and feelings.
I am colorful and spontaneous.
I am full of God's love.
I am fun and outgoing.
I am a survivor.

Who am I?

A smile on my face, I know who I am.

I am the woman with scars, healed and set free.
I am the child abused, but not forgotten.
I am a woman with confidence and not self-doubt.
I am an overcomer; through tears and battles, I
stand high.
I am the child of God, broken but restored together for
His purpose.

In 2018, I began writing poetry again after seeking
the help of a Christian life coach to begin my healing
journey from childhood traumas and relationship
hurts. The poem, "Who Am I," was inspired by time
alone as I journaled through the pain and began to
gain confidence in who I was as a child of God. It was,
in a way, affirmations to myself to help me unpack
painful memories in my mind. Finally, I was able to
release them and let them go.

Bible Verse:

*"But he said to me, 'My grace is sufficient for you, for my
power is made perfect in weakness.' Therefore I will boast
all the more gladly of my weaknesses, so that the power of
Christ may rest upon me"*
(2 Corinthians 12:9, ESV).

When I find myself in a season of weakness, I am reassured that in it all, God will have the glory, and time and time again, God has never failed me when I have prayed and cried out in my weakest moment when life seems to have crumbled all around me. I am, therefore, glad when I am weak. This verse gives me hope and strength.

Prayer:

Dear Abba Father,

Thank You for this day that You have given me. Your promises I speak over my life. I am an overcomer. You have given me life, peace, and joy. You have provided for me always, and I trust you, Lord, even when I don't understand. You go before me and make a way. You created me for a purpose, and I will follow Your voice each step of the way. I will walk in the confidence and authority; I will not be shaken or afraid because I am a child of God. You know who I am, and that alone is enough.

In Jesus name, I pray. Amen.

Reflection

DAY 19:

_____

_____

_____

_____

_____

_____

_____

_____

_____

_____

_____

_____

_____

_____

_____

_____

_____

_____

_____

DAY 20:

DECLARE IT

DAY 20:

DECLARE IT

Believe and declare it now.
I am healed in Jesus' name.
I release the pain of rejection.
I am healed in Jesus' name.
I release the hurts of broken relationships.
I am healed in Jesus' name.
I release all childhood traumas.
I am healed in Jesus' name.
I release the shame of past mistakes.
I am healed in Jesus' name.
I release the bitterness that hardens my heart.
I am healed in Jesus' name.
I release envy that steals my joy today.
I am healed in Jesus' name.

The poem, "Declare It," was inspired by my healing journey when I declared over my life that I was healed. I wrote prayers in my journal that I felt in my spirit would help those who also needed healing through prayer. The blood of Jesus is enough; His love and sacrifice healed us all on the cross. When we believe and declare it, we step into the healing already given to us as Christians. Begin by speaking over your life the truth of the Word of God. Prayer is powerful.

Bible Verse:

*"Praise the Lord, my soul, and forget not all his benefits—
who forgives all your sins and heals all your diseases"
(Psalm 103:2-3 (NIV).*

The Bible is full of testimonies of healings through
prayers and faith. As believers, we have so many
benefits as Children of God, and we have His Word to
help guide us through life. This Bible verse reminds us,
not only to worship our Lord, but reminds us that He
forgives ALL our sins and heals ALL our diseases.

Prayer:

Dear Abba Father,

Thank You for this day. Forgive me for my sins or
any offenses toward anyone. Help me to focus and be
intentional in all areas of my life. Help me to focus on
Your Word and to be mindful of what I am reading so
that I can share Your truths and promises with others.
I declare breakthroughs and healing in my life and
those around me. Thank you for my body, mind, and
soul that is whole and healed through Your Son, Jesus
Christ. I declare healing and peace over my life. I
receive all the blessings and love from heaven above. I
give You all the glory and praise. Let me not forget all
Your benefits over my life.

In Jesus name, I pray. Amen.

Reflection

DAY 20:

_____

_____

_____

_____

_____

_____

_____

_____

_____

_____

_____

_____

_____

_____

_____

_____

_____

DAY 21:

WARRIOR,
KEEP PRAYING

DAY 21:

WARRIOR, KEEP PRAYING

You have been called
To fight for your people.

To stand in the gap
On behalf of those
Hurting, lost, and hopeless.

You are a Prayer Warrior
Called to intercede
So that they may believe.

Go to your secret place
Pray and fast, do not lose faith
We are called for such a
Time as this.

Put on the full Armor of God
Guard your heart and mind
He is our protection and
Peace.

Through years and years of prayers, I understood the
power of not only praying out loud but writing them
down. The Word of God is written, yet we see, like
with Moses to speak, to open our mouths. So, in doing

both, we build up our prayer life with confidence, ready to fight the spiritual attacks of the enemy, each day, as we carry our cross and also intercede for others. To love others is ultimately to pray for them, to love your enemy and bless them, and to help the stranger and to pray protection over them, as well. The poem, "Warrior, Keep Praying" is to encourage the body of Christ to keep praying for one another.

We can never be so busy in life that we cannot pause and pray. When prayer becomes the first thing we do, miracles happen. We win souls for Christ and gain warriors for the kingdom of God. Keep praying, and stay in the fight until the end!

Bible Verse:

"And they overcame him by the blood of the Lamb, and by the word of their testimony; and they loved not their lives unto the death"
(Revelation 12:11, KJV).

When we share with boldness our testimony even through poetry, lives are touched, and God will use anyone with a willing heart. This Bible verse inspires me to keep sharing my testimony through poetry and to tell a story of hope and healing. May we all pray for boldness to pray and speak up.

Prayer:

Dear Abba Father,

Thank You for calling me for such a time as this to stand in the gap for those who need Your love. I am here to help deliver Your people. I have been blessed to bless others.

You move and prepare us. You deliver us for Your purpose. Thank You for choosing me for Your Kingdom's purpose. Lord, here I am; use me and prepare me for the call on my life. I surrender my life to You, Lord. Have Your way in me to be a warrior for Your Kingdom here on Earth. Thank you for the blood of Jesus that gives us the power to do the works set before us.

In Jesus name, I pray. Amen.

Reflection

DAY 21: _____

_____

_____

_____

_____

_____

_____

_____

_____

_____

_____

_____

_____

_____

_____

_____

_____

_____

_____

SOURCE

Stam, Betty Scott. *Betty Scott Stam, A Life of Surrender.*
Revive Our Hearts Blog.

https://www.reviveourhearts.com

STEPHANIE SALINAS ROMAN

ABOUT THE AUTHOR / POET

Stephanie Salinas Roman is a writer and poet who enjoys sharing her work with others. She was born in Texas and raised in a small town in North Carolina. She holds a Bachelor of Science degree in Criminal Justice with a minor in Community & Justice Studies from Guilford College in Greensboro, North Carolina. Faith, family, and friends are very important to Stephanie.

Stephanie has worked in the legal field for over sixteen years. The biggest joy in working with people is serving them and encouraging them through prayer, laughter, or a lending hand. As a young child, Stephanie always enjoyed reading, research, and writing. Her career path gave her the opportunity to use her skills and talents in serving her clients over the years. However, she kept her passion for writing poetry close to her heart with the hopes of one day sharing her passion with the world.

Stephanie enjoys spending time with her husband, Sean, and their children, along with family and friends in the countryside where she finds inspiration to write. As a teenager, poetry was her way of healing from childhood trauma. She now knows it's a gift from God to share her works with those who need healing and those who need to know how to write it out as part of the healing process. Writing can become a catharsis for others as it has for Stephanie. Above all, Mrs. Roman aspires to be a supportive and encouraging woman of God through her words and creativity.

www.ingramcontent.com/pod-product-compliance
Lightning Source LLC
Chambersburg PA
CBHW071800120626
46550CB00002B/858